THE LEHRMAN
PROJECT

The Lehrman Project

THE LEHRMAN PROJECT

EXPERIMENTS IN SUBCONSCIOUS COMMUNICATION

BY STEVEN CLAYSEN

DEEP END BOOKS

The Lehrman Project

First Edition published March 2019

ISBN-13: 978-0-9904973-7-0

Deep End Books
www.stevenclaysen.com

Cover photograph by Dylan O'Donnell
See more of Dylan's work at: www.deography.com

"WORDS ARE EVERYWHERE. WE SPEAK THEM, READ THEM, WRITE THEM, THINK THEM, SEE THEM, TYPE THEM, AND HEAR THEM IN OUR HEAD. IT'S IMPORTANT TO UNDERSTAND THAT ALL WORDS CARRY A VIBRATION FOR THE PERSON WHO SAYS OR THINKS THEM."

-- MICHAEL J. LOSIER

LAW OF ATTRACTION

The Lehrman Project

The Lehrman Project

Also from Steven Claysen:

The Power of Attraction:
How to Apply the Law of Attraction
to Create the Life You Want

Recommended by Steven Claysen:

Prosperity Consciousness
by Fredric Lehrman

The Science of Personal Achievement
by Napoleon Hill

Lessons from the Richest Man Who Ever Lived
by Steven K. Scott

The Lehrman Project

The Lehrman Project

Table of Contents

The Lehrman Project

Author's Note:

I want to thank you for purchasing *"The Lehrman Project: Experiments in Subconscious Communication."*

Since the publication of my book, *"The Power of Attraction,"* I have been inundated with questions like:

"How do I manifest $1,000,000?

"How do I attract the perfect partner?"

"How do I use the Law of Attraction to land my dream job?"

"If this stuff really works, why isn't everyone a millionaire?"

In *"The Lehrman Project: Experiments in Subconscious Communication"* I answer many of these types of questions as I take you through my personal journey of discovery in using subconscious communication and the Law of Attraction to create the life, work, relationships and income I desired.

"The Lehrman Project" contains the exact procedures I followed when I first began learning about the Law of Attraction and subconscious communication. This book can

show you how to use your subconscious mind to help you create the life you desire.

"The Lehrman Project" contains proven steps and strategies on how to create the life you want through learning how to communicate effectively with your own subconscious as well as discovering how to influence others by communicating constructively with their subconscious minds. This book will show you how to harness subconscious communication to help you attain the positive things you are looking for in your relationships, in your financial outcomes, and in your life circumstances, etc.

If any aspect of your life isn't what you hoped it would be, then this book can help you. Thank you again for purchasing *"The Lehrman Project."* May it bring you all the joy and prosperity that you are seeking!

"WE NEED TO STEP BACK AND LISTEN TO HOW OUR MIND COMMUNICATES INTERNALLY ...HOW ONE LEVEL OF OUR MIND TALKS TO ANOTHER LEVEL OF OUR MIND."

-- FREDRIC LEHRMAN

The Lehrman Project

CHAPTER ONE

AN AUSPICIOUS EARTHQUAKE

I was living in Los Angeles when the earthquake hit. It measured only a 3.3 on the Richter Scale and happened around eight o'clock in the morning. You don't usually think of a 3.3 magnitude earthquake as being significant or noteworthy, but this small tremor was powerful enough to change my life forever. Although not an alarming quake, it was forceful enough that the meetings I had planned to attend that morning were postponed, leaving me with extra time on my hands and not much to do.

I had recently been studying Frederic Lehrman's *Prosperity Consciousness* program, looking for a way to improve my financial situation, and I was intrigued by a peculiar procedure Mr. Lehrman refers to as "the Polynesian Mind Model." In his program, Mr. Lehrman outlines a method of communicating subconsciously, not only with our own conscious minds but with the subconscious minds of other people as well. And while these other people are completely unaware of the mental action that we are taking on our part, their subconscious mind is indirectly influenced and, in turn, influences and directs their own conscious mind toward a favorable conclusion. (I'll go into precise detail about how this system operates in the following chapters.)

With the free time I had just been granted by the earthquake, I decided that I would find a quiet room and a comfortable chair and experiment with some of the subconscious mental activities outlined in Mr. Lehrman's program.

The Polynesian Mind Model is abstract and requires that we begin looking at ourselves and, in particular our thought processes, in a new light. By applying the techniques that I am about to reveal to you,

you will begin to see how your mind communicates internally.

You will discover how one level of your mind communicates with another level. This will create for you the ability to communicate more effectively with yourself and allow you to refine your internal dialogue to a degree that will enable you to actually carry out your own mental suggestions without the usual resistance.

The Subconscious Mind and the Physical World

Does the subconscious mind influence and affect the physical world? My father was a physicist involved in the development of the International Space Station. As a sort of hobby, he also loved to experiment with mind powers. At one point in his life, when I was in my early teens, my father determined that he would look at his watch only when the second hand was sweeping the number twelve. It was an investigation in mental training.

"YOU DON'T HAVE TO BE AN ABSOLUTE BELIEVER TO GET RESULTS. YOU JUST HAVE TO BE WILLING TO ENTERTAIN THE POSSIBILITY THAT YOU COULD GET RESULTS."

-- FREDRIC LEHRMAN

Whenever someone asked him the time, he would look at his watch and, invariably, the second hand would be just crossing over the twelve.

"You see that?" he would say, showing us his watch. "See how the second hand is sweeping the twelve? Isn't that something?"

After several years, this little behavior of his became somewhat annoying, (I mean after all, I really just wanted to know the time) but it served as definite proof that his mind was influencing outward conditions in his world. He had no way of knowing, consciously, when the second hand on his watch would be approaching the number twelve, but consistently it would be at the exact moment he looked at his watch.

There were several other mental experiments he would play with, including telekinesis, but this simple act of looking at his watch was enough to convince me at an early age that our subconscious minds can and do influence our circumstances. Without this early experience, I might have found Mr. Lehrman's program a little too peculiar and unconventional to even consider. As it was, I was open-minded enough to make the attempt.

Mr. Lehrman's method, or the Polynesian Mind Model, for implementing suggestions to the subconscious was radically different from anything I had ever come across and I was somewhat skeptical of the process. I wanted to be impartial and give this mind method a fair chance, but the procedure seemed very peculiar and, in all honesty, just plain weird. I had no physical evidence at this point to suggest that these bizarre mental undertakings would be of any value or effectiveness but, as Mr. Lehrman states, "you don't have to be an absolute believer."

I don't mean to scare you off. I only want to explain that the process takes a little getting used to and requires a particularly open-mind. On the positive side, it costs only a small investment of time, and thanks to an earthquake, I had a little time to invest.

The Daniel Experiment

I decided to evaluate this subconscious communication system by trying it out on an associate of mine. We'll call him Daniel (principally because that is his name.)

I met Daniel while we were serving together on the volunteer Board of Directors of an agency in Los Angeles that assists Developmentally Disabled adults. Daniel had a retail enterprise and I had recently started a third-tier marketing company as a side business to my writing career. Daniel and I would sit around and shoot the breeze after our monthly Board meetings and we soon began to realize that we could both benefit from each other's services. Despite our amicable conversations and good intentions, in over three years we had never made time to actually sit down together and work out the details of a business arrangement.

Therefore, Daniel appeared to be the perfect target for my newly acquired subconscious communication technique. Consequently, I sat down in a comfortable armchair away from distractions, put myself in a mild meditative state and spent about a half an hour or so communicating subconsciously with Daniel's subconscious. I must admit it felt awkward and perhaps even silly at the time. This was a definite departure from my normal way of thinking and doing business with people. As skeptical as I was, I gave it my best honest effort. To be truthful, this first attempt felt a little rash and ridiculous, but I went ahead hoping that some good might come out of all this craziness.

I let Daniel know (subconsciously) what my objectives were, how I saw our partnership working and how it would benefit both of us. At one point in our verbal, in-person conversations, Daniel had confided in me that his wife was frustrated with how slowly his business was progressing. Using this information, I subconsciously communicated to Daniel how our partnership would benefit his marriage as well as his business. I presented all of my ideas for a joint business venture and I was very detailed in what I was looking for as well as in what I believed the overall positive results would be for both of us.

After about thirty minutes or so I ended my session with Daniel, or rather, with Daniel's subconscious. It felt a little irrational, mentally discussing all the comprehensive details of a business proposition with someone who wasn't even in the room. Despite all of this, the intriguing aspect of the exercise and the captivating question that fueled my enthusiasm was, 'What if it works?'

I was absolutely amazed at the effectiveness and the results of my first attempt at subconscious communication!

Later that afternoon I telephoned Daniel, and after the usual greetings and updates, I brought up our previous business discussions. This time he was more than just casually interested in setting up a meeting to discuss our ideas. He was extraordinarily enthusiastic and excited. In fact, he wanted to meet that very evening.

"RECOGNIZING AND UNDERSTANDING THIS SUBLIMINAL LEVEL OF COMMUNICATION WILL HAVE A VERY STRONG EFFECT ON ALL OF YOUR BUSINESS PROJECTS."

-- FREDRIC LEHRMAN

"I can't meet tonight, Daniel. I already have other plans," I told him.

"Oh. Yeah. Alright," he replied, a little disappointedly. "How about tomorrow night then?"

We set up a meeting at Daniel's house for the following evening and, despite the positive change I noticed over the phone in Daniel's attitude and enthusiasm, I was still a little concerned that he wouldn't catch the vision of what I had in mind or that he might disagree on or reject some key points of my proposal. Surprisingly, Daniel was not only intrigued by every particular aspect of the proposal but was also extremely anxious to get started immediately toward making this joint venture happen.

This was remarkably different from Daniel's usual offhand response of saying, "Yeah, we should get together sometime." For three years we had talked about developing a partnership and expanding our businesses, but it wasn't until I had prepared Daniel's subconscious mind for the idea of actually doing something that we saw real results in forming an agreement.

I left the meeting that evening encouraged and animated about the business initiative, but I think I was even more amazed and excited about the performance of my new mental business tool, the Polynesian Mind Model.

As I contemplated other applications for Fredric Lehrman's techniques, I thought to myself, 'This could be a life changer!'

In just a matter of months, I discovered how big of a life changer the Polynesian Mind Model would become for both me and my family.

CHAPTER TWO

THE POLYNESIAN MIND MODEL

I have studied and experimented with a number of the many different psychologies of mind that exist in diverse cultures throughout the world. One of the most fascinating and innovative traditions, and one of the most effective in my mind, is the Polynesian tradition which I discovered in Fredric Lehrman's *Prosperity Consciousness* program.

Polynesian psychology views the mind in a very distinct and unusual way. According to Hawaiian and Polynesian philosophies, our mind is divided into three parts. Much like a family, we have a father part, a mother part and a child part. These elements comprise the three different levels and three distinct functions of mind.

The middle level of the mind is referred to as the mother and represents our conscious mind. The mother mind comprises our sense of self. It represents our everyday image of ourselves and our consciousness of the surrounding world. Some of the evident and exclusive characteristics of the middle mind include:

- Decision making.
- A command of language.
- The ability to reason.

The mother portion of the mind is very logical but, surprisingly, it has absolutely no memory. The idea that the conscious mind has no memory is a curious and arresting concept, however, if you think about it, you'll probably agree that it is an accurate description.

Let me give you an illustration.

When you are speaking with another person, you know and understand what you are saying to them. You have the ability to organize your words in a proper sequence to communicate your thoughts. Your voice conveys a logical and reasonable exposition of ideas. Western psychology refers to this linear, logical and verbal part of the brain as left-brain function. It is a rational operation but there are no images or pictures and no memory connected with that voice.

According to the Polynesian Mind Model, if you need to access a memory, you have to retrieve it from the subconscious or the child portion of the mind. If you want to remember a friend's phone number, for example, it isn't in your conscious mind. You need to recover it from a memory stored somewhere in the memory banks of the subconscious mind.

It is the responsibility of the child mind, the subconscious portion of the mind, to keep all of that specific information and data stored away so that when you need it, you will be able to access it.

So, what happens when you can't remember something that you absolutely know that you know? All of us have experienced this type of forgetfulness. You can't remember the name of a particular person but you're certain you know it. Or perhaps you've forgotten the title of a book or a movie. You know it's in your memory somewhere, but it appears to have gotten lost in the dark recesses of your mind. We commonly use the expression, "It's on the tip of my tongue," but we just can't seem to retrieve it from our memory banks. It's like it's been blocked.

So, you let it go and, surprisingly, within minutes it pops back into your conscious awareness. How did that happen? Without you even being aware of what you were doing, you gave an instruction or a command to the child portion of your mind to retrieve that memory. The child mind functions very similar to a librarian who is given instructions to go look through the vast shelves of library books, as if it had a library catalogue card, and retrieve a particular book. The child mind searches through the piles of information stored in your memory bank, locates what it is searching for and comes back with the information. It takes a little time but eventually it will find that memory and give it to the mother portion of the mind.

Experientially, we can see that the memory does work in this manner.

My father often had difficulty remembering names. He would tell himself, "I can't remember that person's name." One day he realized that he was giving very specific instructions to his subconscious mind. He was actually telling himself, "I *can't* remember..." As a result, he didn't remember. Then one day he decided to change his internal dialogue. Instead of saying, "I can't remember that person's name," he would say, "His name will come to me in a minute."

By doing this, he was now instructing his child mind to go retrieve the name he had forgotten and to do it within a minute's time. This made a marked difference in how easily and how quickly he began to remember names. The process works equally well with other memories.

"THE SUBCONSCIOUS IS THERE TO KEEP CHARGE OF THE MEMORIES AND ALSO FOR CERTAIN SUBLIMINAL COMMUNICATION FUNCTIONS."

-- FREDRIC LEHRMAN

A Multiplicity of Personalities

The subconscious mind, the child portion of our brain, is not just a single entity. The child mind is more like a vast array of varying personalities. Fredric Lehrman refers to it as "a whole flock of little children wandering energetically everywhere doing whatever they're doing at the moment with no thought for the future and no thought for the past. They're just active."

Imagine your mind in this way:

Your conscious mind is the mother. Beneath the mother is a group of children, actually, a very large group of children who take every idea handed to them and they just run with it. These children don't function based on logic like the mother mind does. In the Polynesian Mind Model, the subconscious mind functions on a system of emotional logic and feelings that are not necessarily rational. This idea coincides with the concept that "it is the combination of love and thought that create the irresistible force known as the Law of Attraction." [1]

The child mind remembers and reasons by association and comparison and it has perfect memory. It remembers everything, even those things that you think you have forgotten. This is how hypnotherapy is able to access forgotten events from our past. They are forgotten to the conscious mind but not to the subconscious.

The function of the mother mind, our conscious middle mind, is communication, logic and reasoning. The child mind's function is to be responsible for keeping our memories and for certain specific subliminal communication operations that we'll discuss soon.

The higher mind, referred to in the Polynesian culture as the father mind, differs from the mother and child minds in that it has absolute knowledge. It is omniscient.

---

[1] Claysen, Steven, *The Power of Attraction*, Deep End Books, p. 80.

The father mind doesn't reason because it simply knows. The past, present and future are all known by the higher mind. In fact, it knows everything. Our higher self is a connection we make with the all-knowing higher or universal mind.

Each part of the mind operates on a different and a distinct level of energy. The conscious mind works while we are awake. It is active and functioning at a particular energy level when we are alert and aware. When we go to sleep or when our mother mind is occupied and we're not paying attention to the subconscious, the child mind becomes prominent and works at a finer, quieter and more subtle energy level, but very active.

The father mind, or higher level of consciousness, has so much energy it is like looking at the sun. Consciously, we cannot even glimpse it. It is simply too bright. So how do we connect with the higher mind?

In order to access the father portion of the mind, we use the intermediary of the subconscious. The little children in our subconscious mind have no fear of the higher mind with its tremendous power and light. They simply don't know any better.

According to the Polynesian Mind Model, when we pray, the mother mind, our conscious awareness, is actually talking to the child mind, our subconscious. We make a request for a blessing, guidance, instruction, health, or some other specific result and the child portion of our mind wanders off to talk to the father mind and to ask for knowledge or healing or some change that can be brought into conscious existence. This result comes the same way a memory comes to us.

We are not consciously aware of what is happening, but the children aspect of the subconscious mind goes off to do the work for us. It is as if these little children venture out to talk to their father and then come back with a message for their mother. This is how we converse within our own minds.

When you need to deal with other people, the Polynesian Mind Model suggests that you first talk to your own subconscious mind. Then, while you are asleep or while you're not paying attention, independent of your conscious awareness, your subconscious mind will actually communicate your thoughts, ideas and feelings to the subconscious mind of the person you are wanting to interact with. It's like it sends a delegation ahead of you and the two subconscious groups communicate and negotiate with each other.

They then take to the conscious mind the memories, the images, and the impulses which will actually get the two minds to meet, to agree, to see things eye-to-eye.

There Are No Accidents

Isn't it mysterious and intriguing to see how our lives are directed? Do you ever wonder why you meet certain people at certain times in your life?

"IF I WANT TO MAKE A BUSINESS PROJECT HAPPEN, I FIRST OF ALL TALK TO MY SUBCONSCIOUS."

-- FREDRIC LEHRMAN

Perhaps you've noticed how differently you feel around different people. Some people may make you feel comfortable and relaxed. Other people make you nervous or anxious. Some people you connect with immediately and trust them completely. Other people generate feelings of fear and resistance for no apparent reason.

It is interesting to consider that other people are simultaneously reacting to you in a similar fashion without you saying or doing anything. I have a good friend by the name of Jeff who moved away, then met and fell in love with a woman who claimed to know me. Not only did she claim to know me, but she made it very clear that she didn't think very highly of me. When Jeff mentioned this to me, I racked my brain to think of where I had even met this woman and what had I possibly done to create a bad impression on her.

It was several weeks before I remembered being at a conference with this woman. We were introduced in the lobby but beyond that, we had no interaction whatsoever. On some level of mind, she had had a negative experience in meeting me. We can change how people respond to us by changing how we communicate internally.

(On a humorous side note, I wrote to this woman explaining that I understood that she didn't think very highly of me. She wrote back and told me I was wrong; she didn't think of me at all.)

Recognizing and understanding this subliminal level of communication will have a very influential effect on your business projects, personal relationships and financial interests just as it has had on mine. Once we calm our noisy mental chatter and listen to how one level of our mind communicates internally with another level of our mind, we are granted the possibility of talking to ourselves in a manner that is much more effective and profitable. By refining our inner dialogue, we will find ourselves carrying out our own mental suggestions with little or no resistance.

The Polynesian Mind Model accepts that there are no accidents. Our subconscious minds have contacted each other long in advance to arrange meetings, encounters or get-togethers where our conscious minds can enter into the same space at the same time and identify and recognize each other.

All of this is nothing more than theory. It cannot be proven but it can be experienced as I have experienced it. I have used the Polynesian Mind Model to create business deals, to obtain employment, to improve relationships, to manifest money and even to get a good parking space at the market.

Whenever I want to make something happen in my life, whether it is a business deal, repairing a relationship or simply paying off a credit card, I talk to my subconscious before taking any action. I want to be certain that I am communicating with the subconscious of the people I want to deal with in order to clear the way for the negotiations that will follow in real time. This has proven to be the most efficient and effective way for me to accomplish anything in the conscious realm.

Everything depends on how well we communicate within ourselves.

"I'VE BEEN TESTING IT FOR MYSELF FOR OVER 20 YEARS AND I RELY ON IT ABSOLUTELY. I KNOW IT'S THE MOST EFFICIENT WAY FOR ME TO GET ANYTHING DONE."

-- FREDRIC LEHRMAN

CHAPTER THREE

SUBCONSCIOUS PUPPIES—MENTAL PROPERTIES

Since everything depends on how effectively we communicate within ourselves, it is imperative that we master our inner dialogue. Families have problems. Fathers and mothers don't always see eye-to-eye. Children don't always listen or obey. Just as every family can have difficulty communicating effectively, we can also have problems with our internal communication.

Something you've probably observed in your life is that there are moments when everything goes well. Life just runs smoothly. There are other times when you find resistance everywhere. It comes in waves. Everything is succeeding and advancing and then, all of a sudden, nothing is.

This is not accidental. These changes are created by your internal dialogue. If you are sure about what you want and have no resistance to it—and your communication between your conscious mind and your subconscious mind is clear—then you will move forward in obtaining your desire. If you have doubts about what you want, if you're uncertain about a course of action, then you'll hesitate, and you won't move forward, or you'll delay moving forward with your desire.

The subconscious works in a very similar fashion. It needs clear and certain instruction. Our subconscious mind is eager to please and wants nothing more than to connect with us and carry out our desires and wishes. Fredric Lehrman compares the subconscious mind to an energetic little puppy dog. A little puppy just wants to give love and get love in return.

Most people know what is like to have a puppy at home and they understand what happens when that puppy doesn't get enough attention. Puppies have boundless amounts of energy. They can't sit still. They have to be active and they are constantly seeking attention.

If you fail to give a puppy the attention it is seeking, the puppy will escalate its plea for attention. So, the little puppy will jump up on your bed in the morning and begin to lick your face or bite at your hands to wake you up so that you can give it attention. That is what it wants. If you don't give the puppy the love and attention it is seeking, then you will notice that the next day it will increase and heighten its efforts.

One morning you may wake up to find the puppy at the foot of your bed chewing up your slippers. The puppy has been chewing on your slippers all night in an attempt to connect with you.

The chewed-up slippers are just a metaphor for disasters of varying magnitude that occur in our lives. Sometimes we look around us and we see chewed-up slippers everywhere. Our business may be in disorder. Our personal relationships may be suffering. We may be having difficulties with our children or a neighbor or a co-worker. What we are actually experiencing is a communication break-down internally between our conscious mind and our subconscious mind. The subconscious mind is running amuck and chewing up all our slippers in order to get our attention.

The attention that our subconscious needs from us is recognition and clear instructions. If your outer world is breaking down, if there are chewed-up slippers everywhere in your life, then there is some lack of clarity in communication between your conscious mind and your subconscious mind. The good news is that we can change what is happening around us by changing our internal dialogue.

When you train a puppy, you give it love and recognition and you give it clear instruction. You show the puppy exactly what is expected of it, practice with it and you reward it with a treat whenever it meets those expectations. As the puppy learns what you expect, it becomes happy being obedient to your wishes.

It may be strange to consider, but all of this is already happening within your own mind continually whether you are aware of it or not. You have all these little children that you are responsible for. These children will be well-behaved and obedient if you give them the attention that they so earnestly seek and desire. The way you give attention to these children is through internal dialogue, through meditation and through prayer.

Mr. Lehrman explains that "you don't have to be an absolute believer to get results. You just have to be willing to entertain the possibility that you could get results." Simply believing is enough to tip the scales—as it did in my case with my friend Daniel—and then you will begin to experience the changes that you are seeking and striving for. Once you begin to witness these changes, you will believe even more, and the changes will occur more quickly and with greater ease. Change will then happen faster, and you'll be even more convinced, which will accelerate greater change.

The Lehrman Project

"THE QUEST FOR TRUTH IS ESSENTIALLY AN EXPERIMENT."

-- STEVEN CLAYSEN

Imagine that you are planting a seed in cerebral soil, in your thoughts. This seed is your belief. You place the seed in the soil. You can't be certain whether it will germinate and grow or not, but you plant it anyway. Then you wait, watch and hope. If you do no more than accept the possibility that these subconscious exercises of the mind *could* work, then you have planted your seed.

But planting is more than simply sowing a seed in soil. It requires active attention and effort in cultivating, nourishing, and even harvesting. Though the potential for harvest lies within the seed, desired results come only through physical, mental, and spiritual energy and efforts on our part.

The quest for truth is essentially an experiment. A valuable seed, or correct principle, is one which, if properly understood and nourished, will grow and produce good fruit in its season. In this case, the seed is not some vague philosophical abstraction; rather, the seed is something very specific, a mental process for communicating and receiving our personal desires.

An idea needs nourishment just as much as the physical body needs nourishment. Mental activity requires the same attention as its physical counterpart. Mental strength and ability do not come instantaneously. They must be nourished and cared for just like a seed in a garden. Results, the harvest of our mental seeds, grow within our mind's soil quietly and imperceptibly.

A good seed properly nourished will always produce a rich harvest in its proper season. However, you may also notice that a few unwelcomed weed seeds fall into your fertile cerebral soil. As you begin these subconscious activities, Mr. Lehrman suggests that you may encounter some interesting surprises.

As you begin to change and develop your mental pattern and processes, you will discover parts of your subconscious that, until you re-educate them, will remain loyal to your old belief system. The time it takes for your mental seed to produce its harvest, in other words, the time it takes to get results from these subconscious communication exercises, depends on how much certainty you have in the process. You need to be aware and conscious of any doubt.

Mental Properties

Mr. Lehrman suggests that this process of planting new mental seeds is like buying investment property. Imagine you were to purchase an apartment complex with twenty-five units. You want to improve the value of the property by repairing and upgrading the building. Of course, there are tenants (your old thinking patterns) who have been living there for years. You visit the property and discover the reason it is not as valuable as it should be is because the tenants (your thoughts) are not living in a very effective or prosperous way. There is garbage in the halls and on the grounds. No one has been taking care of needed repairs. You realize that simply painting the outside of the building won't help because so much is in disrepair on the inside.

"EVERY THOUGHT, EVERY EMOTION, EVERY WORD SPOKEN, EVERY ACTION ON YOUR PART IS A SEED SOWN."

-- STEVEN CLAYSEN

Accordingly, you notify the tenants that you are going to be improving the (mental) property and making changes that will require you to increase the rent but that everyone will be better off in the end. A lot of the tenants are going to come forward to protest and complain that they don't want you to raise the rent. They been living comfortably in your mind for years and they don't want you to make any improvements or changes. They just want everything to stay the way it is.

That is how your mind works as well. It wants to stay the way it is. For change to occur, you need to take over like a new landlord and announce that you are going to make improvements to your mind and any thoughts who wish to stay are going to have to function at a higher level of thinking. You will need to raise the rent on your previous thoughts, but it will be worth it.

The thoughts that don't want to stay will move out, but they will come forward and try to protest these improvements and changes in your thought process. When you make a positive change or begin a new program in your life, you can expect to run into your own resistance—just as I did with my thoughts and feelings of foolishness during my own first attempt to communicate subconsciously with Daniel. Your resistant tenants may even get a little loud at times. It will take some commitment on your part to work through the resistance and emerge where all your thoughts are in agreement.

Once you do, you will begin to experience rapid change and improvement in your life.

We no longer live in a world based on material limitations. Instead our world is determined by the mental concepts we hold in our heads. Your future wealth and opportunity are determined more by the way that you think and not by your current assets.

CHAPTER FOUR

THE ART OF SUBCONSCIOUS COMMUNICATION

Brian Tracey wrote that "every change in your life will come about as the result of your mind colliding with a new idea." I had been uncertain and felt silly on my first attempt at communicating subconsciously to set up a favorable meeting with Daniel. You can imagine, I'm sure, the awkwardness of gathering and talking to little children that only exist in the subconscious mind, telling them how much you love and appreciate them, thanking them for all they've done over a lifetime, and then instructing them to carry ideas from one's own subconscious mind to the subconscious of another individual. It was bizarre, to say the least. But in the back of my mind I kept thinking, 'What if this works?'

I was utterly astonished and pleasantly surprised to witness just how well it did work. Perhaps, as I explain to you the process that I used you will understand why it felt foolish and even puerile. I ask only that you keep an open mind and see for yourself the fantastic results and possibilities associated with this peculiar and curious form of internal communication.

Let me begin by explaining the steps I went through with my first attempt at subconscious communication with Daniel. As I mentioned earlier, I sat in a comfortable armchair, shut my eyes and entered into a mild meditative state of mind. In other words, I relaxed my thinking and shut out all outward distractions. I was alone and knew I wouldn't be interrupted. I began an internal monologue that lasted for thirty minutes or so. This will be an abbreviated re-telling but it went something like this.

"Hello children. Please gather around. I need to speak with you about something." I repeated this request several times in differing phrases just to be certain that those children were paying attention. After all, this was the first time I had spoken to them in this manner. (Perhaps you can understand why I felt a little silly at this point. Please bear with me.)

"I want you all to know how much I appreciate you and all that you do for me. I am very grateful to you for sustaining me and supporting me. I am thankful for everything you have done for me over my lifetime. Thank you for keeping me alive, for seeing to it that my heart keeps beating and my lungs continue to breathe. I love and appreciate you for all that you do for me."

I have come to realize that gratitude is one of the greatest tools for creating enormous abundance, wealth and success in life. In my book, *The Power of Attraction*, I stated that, "If you are thankful for having something it will show up in your life…. Gratitude is a thought pattern strongly tied to an emotion and it will take root, blossoming eventually into acts, events and circumstances that will bear the fruit of opportunity and abundance." [2] Expressing gratitude to your own subconscious mind for supporting your life systems and providing you with all you need to survive is an extremely powerful and positive technique for improving your life circumstances.

Consequently, for several minutes I rehearsed an extensive list of the things I felt grateful for in my life to my subconscious children. After this, I began my request.

"So, I want to thank you for all that you have done for me and I want to ask a favor of you. I need you to take a message to the children of Daniel's subconscious mind and explain to them that it would be very beneficial for the two of us to meet and discuss specific plans for how we could create a business partnership. I need you to convince Daniel's subconscious mind that this partnership will not only benefit our business venture together but will also

---

[2] Claysen, Steven. *The Power of Attraction*, Deep End Books, pp. 87, 99.

provide us both improved results in our separate businesses."

At this point I began to review the different components of my business proposal, informal as it was, to my subconscious children. I asked these children to tell Daniel's children that our combined efforts would be much more productive than our separate individual efforts could ever be.

I communicated to Daniel's subconscious mind the different aspects of the plan that I was hoping he would recognize and accept as valuable components of our enterprise. As I mentioned earlier, I even had my subconscious children explain to his subconscious children how our joint efforts could also improve his relationship with his wife.

I wanted Daniel to be very clear about how he would profit from our business venture and I discussed extensively all the benefits I could see for Daniel with the children of my subconscious.

The Lehrman Project

"IF YOU ARE THANKFUL FOR HAVING SOMETHING IT WILL SHOW UP IN YOUR LIFE."

-- STEVEN CLAYSEN

My approach was not to convince myself about the benefits of a partnership, but to convince Daniel, accordingly much of the mental effort I employed was to make Daniel aware of how he could benefit from all of this.

After I had repeated my ideas and instructions several times—again, just to make certain that everyone was listening—I then thanked my subconscious children and instructed them, "Now go and present these ideas to Daniel's subconscious children. Help them see the value of these concepts and the importance of acting on them as quickly as possible."

(I did, initially, use a lot of repetition in my requests and in my expressions of gratitude and love. I wasn't certain how much mental exertion was required to produce an effective outcome. Over time I have been able to become more succinct and precise in my requests to my subconscious children.)

It was simple enough and I felt good about the attempt I had made. I allowed a few hours to go by before

I telephoned Daniel to asked him if he wanted to meet and discuss some ideas for a joint venture. As I stated earlier, Daniel was ready and eager to meet that very evening.

When we did meet, every idea that I had communicated subconsciously to Daniel's subconscious he had accepted without hesitation and a prosperous joint venture ensued.

Securing Employment

I was born in a small farming town near Columbus, Ohio. Life in Los Angeles was a stark contrast to the uncrowded, open and peaceful community of my childhood. I was doing very well for myself as a writer in L.A., but events were dictating that a change would be necessary.

My son was attending a middle school where students carried knives and got into frequent fights. There was a drive-by shooting at my daughter's elementary school. As difficult as it is for me to fathom any type of shooting beyond self-defense, I had an extremely difficult time wrapping my head around the idea that anyone would want to shoot up a grade school playground. The tipping point for me came when the body of a murder victim was dumped in the bushes just two houses down from mine.

I determined at that moment to move my family out of Los Angeles, and I began looking for a more suitable environment in a community where life would be a little more peaceful. I quit my job and moved my family to a small farming town back east. I figured that I would have to commute to a larger town to find work, but I had already been spending two and a half hours a day commuting to and from my job in Los Angeles. So, I wasn't concerned that I might need to travel to another city.

I spent my first week just looking at various companies in the area, meeting with executives but not really looking for a position. On Friday, a friend suggested I look into a growing company about a forty-five-minute drive from where I was now living. I made an appointment to meet with the owner on Monday morning.

I told my sister in L.A. about my upcoming interview. She kindly reminded me that, "You never get the first job you apply for."

Monday morning arrived and I began driving to my appointment. It was then that I remember Fredric Lehrman's subconscious communication program. I couldn't very well shut my eyes and enter into a meditative state while I was driving down the highway, but I thought I could still talk to my subconscious children. The commute was not on an overcrowded freeway like it had been in Los Angeles, but was, rather, down a country lane through flowing cornfields and along the shore of a pristine lake which was much more conducive to creating a peaceful state of mind. I hadn't sat down to do a full session of subconscious communication since that first attempt with Daniel, but I was certainly willing to give it another try with so much at stake.

The mental exercise session on my drive into the city went very similar to my first attempt at subconscious communication. I gathered the children around me, thanked them for all their support and assistance and told them how much I loved and appreciated them. (I even apologized for not speaking to them as often as I should have.) I then rehearsed to them all the benefits I could provide for my potential new employer. I reviewed the benefits I would receive as well as the services and value I would deliver. I provided my subconscious children with all the reasons I could think of that would make me a winning candidate for this job. I then instructed them to carry this message to Carl, the owner of the company.

As it turned out, my meeting was not only with Carl but also with his wife, Faye (a co-owner in his business,) and with two other executives. As I laid out my qualifications for the position and they laid out their expectations for their potential new employee, it became apparent that what I had to offer was not what they were looking for. Once I recognized this, I apologized that I had not researched their company properly before making an appointment with them. I also apologized for wasting their time and politely told them that I did not think I was the right candidate for the position.

I left feeling disappointed, partly at not getting the job but also at having to admit that my sister was right— you don't get the first job you apply for.

The following morning, I received a phone call from Carl asking if I could meet with him for a second interview on Wednesday morning. I told Carl that I was willing to meet with him, but I was confused.

"I didn't think you had a position for me," I told him.

"Well, we've created one," was Carl's reply.

On Wednesday morning Carl, Faye and their other two executives laid out the duties and responsibilities of the new position that was tailor-made for the abilities and talents I had to offer. The pay was less than what I had made in Los Angeles, but the lower cost of living made up the difference.

Not only could I now prove my sister wrong, I could also bring additional proof that Fredric Lehrman's program for subconscious communication can bring us the life that we are actively seeking.

As a side note, after our interview, Carl asked me where I was living. I gave him the name of the town and he told me that his company was opening an office there. I asked him the specific location and discovered that the office building was located just two blocks from my new home. It opened within six months of my initial interview and I was given an office on the second floor with a large window that overlooked the pristine lake and flowing cornfields.

I did not forget to thank my subconscious children.

The Lehrman Project

CHAPTER FIVE

IMPROVING PERSONAL RELATIONSHIPS SUBCONSCIOUSLY

On a beautiful afternoon, shortly after settling in at my new office, my wife called me on the telephone to ask if her recently divorced sister and two nieces could come to live with us. I instantly received an overwhelming impression that this was a very bad idea and I tried to talk my wife out of it but a part of me kept asking, 'What if it was your sister who needed help. Wouldn't you want your wife to be open and agreeable to supporting you? How can you deny her the same help?' Very plainly against my better judgment, I acquiesced.

They say always trust your gut feelings. I wish I had listened. Shortly after my sister-in-law and her two daughters moved in with us, trouble began. Her children fought and bickered with my children. My children felt that their home, their personal space, had been invaded. Everyone blamed each other for anything wrong that happened. I defended my children while my wife sided with her sister and nieces. Over the next six months tensions escalated. I'll spare you the sordid details, but life became intolerable and my relationship with my wife deteriorated with the speed of a bullet train.

One day I left my office at noon and decided to take a walk down an abandoned railroad track that ran alongside the office building. (At least, I hoped it was abandoned.) I thought about the feelings my wife and I shared when we had first met. I remembered so many of the good times we had experienced together. I saw it all disintegrating right in front of me and felt powerless to stop it. But I had to do something.

As I walked along the track, I summoned my subconscious children to gather around again. After asking for their attention, thanking them for their continuous support and expressing my love to them, I began to ask them to take a message to the children of my wife's subconscious mind.

I asked them to communicate all the deep feelings of affection and love that I had for my wife. I asked them to convey those memories of happier, more loving and pleasant times to her. I asked them to let her know how much I still cared for her and how much she meant to me. I asked them to share the concerns I felt over our present situation and how unhappy I was that we were at odds with each other.

I thanked my subconscious children and sent them off to deliver my message as I headed back to the office to finish my afternoon's work.

Shortly before five, I noticed my wife's car pull into the parking lot outside my office. She came upstairs and sat in a chair across from my desk. I could tell immediately that something was different. Her countenance had changed. She sat quietly while I finished up some paperwork, but she never took her eyes off of me. She wasn't just looking at me; she was staring with a gaze that reminded me of some adolescent schoolgirl watching her teen idol rock star at work.

I laughed. "Why are you looking at me like that?" I asked her.

"Like what?"

"I don't know. Kind of like a schoolgirl, I guess. What are you doing here anyway?"

"I just wanted to pick you up from work."

I reminded her that we lived only two blocks away and I could easily have walked home. We went downstairs to the car together and got inside. She continued to stare starry-eyed at me.

Smiling, I asked: "What's gotten into you?"

"Nothing. I just feel, I don't know, I just feel so close to you right now and I want to be with you."

I asked her if she wanted to go out to dinner. She did so we drove to a town that had more than just a burger joint and were seated at a small table. She continued her love-struck gazing and told me that she felt such a powerful affection toward me at that moment. So over dinner, I explained Fredric Lehrman's process of subconscious communication and how I had used it to convey my deepest feelings for her. My wife is particularly superstitious, so I spent the remainder of the evening explaining to her that I am not a warlock and I did not cast a spell on her, although, I have to admit, the results were exceptionally similar.

I discovered in no uncertain terms that subconscious communication can convey feelings as well as thoughts and that injured and battered relationships can be mended and healed using this technique. Despite the rapid change in my wife's demeanor, everything in our life together did not suddenly come up roses.

"WHATEVER YOU EXPECT, WITH CONFIDENCE, BECOMES YOUR OWN SELF-FULFILLING PROPHECY."

-- BRIAN TRACEY

Her sister continued to be a problem even after she eventually moved out. All of us suffered from the experience but establishing a more solid foundation of feelings between myself and my wife, through subconscious communication, endowed us with the strength and the determination to weather the storm together.

Changing your relationships requires expanding your ideas and imagination about the person you are and the person you would like to become. It is about rising above your current situation, with its limitations and problems, and seeing yourself living the life you desire. This type of thinking requires practice. The Polynesian Mind Model with its concept of three minds, the mother mind or conscious mind, the child mind or subconscious and the father mind or the superconscious, is essential to changing your thinking and changing your life.

In developing effective relationships with a spouse, a co-worker, your children or anyone else for that matter, your commission is to monitor, manage and control your thinking. One of the paramount qualifications you can acquire in this life is the ability to effectively communicate, negotiate, influence, and persuade other people. This ability is characterized by an elevated compassion, sensitivity and awareness of the thoughts, feelings, motivations, and desires of the people around you.

Stress is inevitable. Problems are constant and never-ending. Failure and disappointment happen to all of us. Unfortunately, it is easy to slip into the habit of criticizing and complaining. The only thing we can truly control is how we respond to stressful events.

Keep your words and thoughts clearly and completely focused on the type of relationship you really want. At the same time, you must refuse to think about what you don't want. Your primary intention for strengthening a relationship should always be to make positive subconscious communication a habitual way of thinking.

CHAPTER SIX

A TEAM OF MENTAL AMBASSADORS

I was listening to *The Science of Personal Achievement* by Napoleon Hill one afternoon. Mr. Hill mentions in this program that he has, what he calls, a roving ambassador. Curiously enough, this is not a physical person existing in the real world but is, instead, a mental character working in Mr. Hill's subconscious mind. My experiences with the subconscious mind led me to investigate the powers and possibilities of having my own roving ambassador.

The first thing I discovered was that the roving ambassador was only one member of a team of mental ambassadors that Napoleon Hill used to create his overwhelming success. To keep it simple and easier for my mind to digest, I decided to start unpretentiously with just my one roving ambassador.

In *The Science of Personal Achievement,* Mr. Hill explains the purpose of a mental roving ambassador. His roving ambassador exists to take care of the mundane details of life so that Mr. Hill doesn't need to worry about them. He is in charge of the busy-ness of living and working and existing on this planet.

For instance, one of the duties Mr. Hill has assigned to his roving ambassador is finding a convenient parking place in front of the bank whenever Mr. Hill needs to be there. That isn't everything this ambassador is charged with, but it certainly seems simple enough and easy enough to experiment with and prove. Therefore, I decided to create my own roving ambassador and set him to work for me.

To make it easier to address instructions to his roving ambassador, Mr. Hill gave him a name. It was a combination of his own last name and his wife's maiden-name. My last name and my wife's maiden name offer no combinations that would be a suitable name for a roving ambassador, so at my wife's suggestion, I combined our middle names.

My middle name is Richard, hers is Lee. And so, Mr. Rich Lee became my roving ambassador. (The other choice was Hard Lee and that *hardly* seemed appropriate.) I wanted to start simply and just experiment with the concept to see if it actually worked. Consequently, Rich Lee's only task, at first, was to get me a parking space in front of the bank as Napoleon Hill had mentioned. The bank in our town is in a little strip mall with inadequate parking and I figured that these conditions would provide the acceptable means to test Mr. Hill's concept of having the subconscious mind take care of the little conveniences in the physical world.

Consequently, I gathered my subconscious children around me one evening and, as usual, thanked them for all they do for me and told them how much I love and appreciate them. Then I explained to them that Rich Lee would be going to work as my roving ambassador. Although I only intended to try the idea of a roving ambassador with getting a good parking spot, I laid out various other duties that I expected Rich to eventually undertake for me. I again thanked those mental children and sent them on their way to take care of me.

Then, on the following pay-day, I told Rich Lee that I needed a parking space right in front of the bank. As I pulled into the strip mall parking lot, I could see every spot in front of the bank was already occupied. Just as I was about to drive off to some remote corner of the parking lot, a car immediately in front of the bank pulled out and opened a spot for me.

This wasn't life changing by any means. It wasn't as significant a securing employment or mending a relationship, but it certainly was convenient. It was also kind of fun. And, for those of you who think (rightfully so) that this was merely a coincidence, over the months that followed, it proved to work about eighty percent of the time. There may have been moments where I doubted on some level or maybe it just doesn't always work. Whatever the case, it's satisfying and amusing to have a convenient parking place whenever I go to the bank, even if it only happens eighty percent of the time.

So now, whenever I leave work or my home, I tell my roving ambassador, "I'm going to need a parking space right in front of—" where ever it is I am headed.

One evening, near Christmas time, I had to go to the market and, although I knew the parking lot would be crowded, I forgot to instruct Rich Lee to find me a space in front of the store. As I approached the parking lot I thought, "Oh no. I forgot to ask for a good parking space!" I began to tell Rich Lee that I needed a place to park and, because I was late in asking, anything near the store would be fine. But then I stopped myself. Why should I compromise? If I really believed in subconscious communication, I should be able to have any parking place I ask for. I subsequently told Rich Lee that I needed the parking place directly in front of the door.

"WHATEVER IS IMPRESSED IS EXPRESSED."

-- ARISTOTLE

Needless to say, the parking lot was jammed. Cars were moving back and forth searching for a place to park. I entered the parking lot and, just as I approached the store, the car parked directly in front of the door pulled out, opening not only a convenient parking space but the exact spot I had asked Rich Lee to secure for me.

When I explained the concept of a roving ambassador to my employer, Carl, he was skeptical and doubtful, so I began sending him text photos of my car parked expediently in front of the bank almost every payday. Eventually, Carl asked me why I was wasting Rich Lee's abilities on just getting parking spaces.

Carl was right. It was time to expand my roving ambassador's duties. I put him in charge of all the little conveniences of life. I also set up and gave Rich Lee charge over a team of mental ambassadors who specialize in diverging aspects of my life and livelihood. All of them were given names that were meaningful to me.

If you are curious enough to discover whether a team of ambassadors could help you with your life and livelihood, then I suggest you give them names that will be meaningful and powerful for you.

My team of ambassadors looks like this:

Rich Lee:	Roving Ambassador
Daniel:	Health Ambassador
Solomon:	Financial/Career Ambassador
George:	Relationship Ambassador
Albert:	Mental Ambassador
Enoch:	Spiritual Ambassador

I've already shown how Mr. Hill and how I came up with the names for our roving ambassadors. Let me explain the meaning behind the names and the job descriptions of the rest of my ambassador team.

I chose the name Daniel from Daniel in the Old Testament who refused to eat the king's 'junk food' but preferred the healthier choices of the traditional food of his upbringing. He seemed like a strong character for the namesake of my health ambassador. Also, at the time I created my health ambassador, I was going through *The*

Daniel Plan, a health program designed by Dr. Daniel Amen, Rick Warren and Mark Hyman. For me, Daniel was the obvious choice for a health ambassador.

Daniel's job is to assist me to make healthy lifestyle choices and to heal my physical body whenever it encounters disease or any form of malady. Weight control, exercise activities, and healthy food choices are all entrusted to Daniel. [3]

I chose Solomon for the name of my financial and career ambassador after listening to *Lessons from the Richest Man Who Ever Lived* by Steven K. Scott. In this program Steven Scott explains that King Solomon, even by today's standards, would be the richest man who ever lived on this planet. I could not think of anyone better than

---

[3] Disclaimer: Please note that I do NOT use my health ambassador in lieu of expert medical advice. I always consult a qualified physician and recommend the same for others. Daniel's job is to work in conjunction with expert advice.

the wisest, richest man who ever lived to be my financial and career ambassador. [4]

Solomon's primary concern is increasing my income and securing my career. It's a fluid position that changes based on different business ventures. Solomon is always seeking new opportunities to help me expand my career and multiply my income.

The name of my relationship ambassador was the most difficult to come up with until I remembered a friend who seemed to have an excellent relationship with his wife and had even recorded a few audio programs on successful relationships. His name was George.

I turn to George when I need help in personal or business relationships. Any hardship between myself and another person I have dealings with is given over to George.

My father has the same I.Q. as Albert Einstein and Stephen Hawking. All three of them have incredible

---

[4] Disclaimer: Your financial ambassador should not replace expert financial advice or career planning.

mental powers. I chose Albert because Stephen might be too confusing as it is so similar to my own name. My father's name could produce issues from my childhood unrelated to his intelligence. Albert seemed the obvious choice for a mental ambassador.

Albert's job is to expand my mind and improve my education. He helps me grasp intellectual concepts and makes them understandable and relatable to my current situations.

The name Enoch, my spiritual ambassador, is from another Old Testament character. He was, I believe, a powerful spiritual leader. Therefore, I took his name for my spiritual ambassador.

Enoch assists in the spiritual development of my soul and in the religious practices I attempt to undertake in my life. He strengthens my relationship with God.

There is nothing that says you need to have the same titles, job descriptions or names for your own ambassadors. Only you know your life and where you need assistance. You can determine the number of ambassadors you require and give them any type of task that you feel will benefit your own situation and circumstances. Nothing is set in stone. Your mind can be as fluid as you would like it to be.

As I worked with my ambassadors little-by-little, and my confidence in the process grew, I began turning over larger projects for them to assist with. I cannot physically prove that it has helped me succeed in any venture, but, as Mr. Lehrman stated, I have been using these techniques for years and I rely on them absolutely. Your openness to these concepts and ideas will determine the level of your own success with them.

Perhaps you are thinking that watching the second hand of your watch sweep across the number twelve or getting the best parking space at the bank seems pretty inconsequential. Maybe you are thinking that you have real problems in the real world that can't be solved by simply getting a better parking spot. The purpose of these exercises is not to get you the best parking place in town. Their purpose is to create awareness and to produce results that are evidentiary proof of your own mental powers.

If your subconscious mind can provide you with the perfect parking place, then it can also provide you with the money that you need. It can create for you the perfect job that you are seeking. It can place you in the ideal relationship or it can transform the relationship you are already in. Glancing at the second-hand on your watch or seeking the idyllic parking spot is simply a training exercise to convince you that *all of your desires*, including the less tangible ones, are within your grasp.

It is simply a matter of convincing your own mind that you can be, do or have anything that you truly desire.

The Lehrman Project

CHAPTER SEVEN

PROSPERITY AND THE SUBCONSCIOUS

I have had many people ask me, "If this stuff works, then why isn't everyone a millionaire?" Why indeed! The question itself opens up an entire realm of possibility which can be examined on many levels.

It may seem strange, but some people may not want to be millionaires.

A friend once told me that if a person earns $25,000 a year and works for 40 years, that person will have earned one million dollars. I had been working for about twenty years at that time, making well over $25,000 annually so I went home and jokingly asked my wife, "Where's my half million dollars?" The point is, people can become millionaires but without proper money management they may never even notice it.

Some people can never get over their own doubts that something as simple as changing their inner dialogue could make a meaningful difference.

Believe it or not, for some people the mental activity is not worth the physical benefit or advantage.

There are other people who, on a certain level, do not believe they are worthy or that they have any intrinsic value. Subconsciously shunning money is how they deal with their feelings of unworthiness and inadequacy. They don't value themselves and therefore are not open to the value prosperity would bring to them.

Other people have a learned reaction based on the idea that money is 'the root of all evil.' It is, actually, the love of money that constitutes the root of all evil. The idea is, nonetheless, ingrained so deeply in some people's minds that subconsciously they reject wealth and prosperity even though they outwardly believe they want it.

All of these concerns and mental blockages to the flow of wealth, abundance and prosperity can be overcome through meaningful internal dialogue. It takes mental effort and a strong desire, but it is possible to correct and improve our thinking. We can improve our mental property by evicting the thoughts that refuse to live at a higher, healthier state of awareness.

A woman once came to me, we'll call her Susan because, again, that was her name. She told me she wanted to be wealthy and had been working for decades but could never rise above the level of income that she considered 'just getting by.' Opportunities for increased income would present themselves in her life but they never seemed to pan out.

I invited her to do one of Fredric Lehrman's *Prosperity Consciousness* exercises with me. She consented. I will walk you through the same exercise that I performed with her. (As this is a meditation exercise, you may want to have someone else read this portion of the book to you so that you can get the full effect of the activity. If you do, you should be seated in a comfortable chair, in a room where you will be uninterrupted, and put yourself in a meditative frame of mind. Or, if you simply want to read about it, that works as well.) I invited Susan to sit in a comfortable chair and close her eyes. After helping her to relax, I then conducted the following exercise with her.

Imagine you are at home in your living room. You are getting ready for your day when you hear a knock on the front door. You go to the door and open it, but no one is there. Instead, you find a large leather trunk left on your doorstep. It is clearly labeled with your name. There is no doubt that this trunk is meant for you.

You take hold of one of the straps on the side of the trunk and drag it into your living room. The trunk is extremely heavy. Again, you note that the trunk is labeled and intended for you, so you undo the latch on the front of the trunk and open the lid.

You discover that the trunk is full of neatly wrapped hundred-dollar bills. It is more money than you have ever seen, and it is entirely yours. You don't know exactly how much is there, but you know you will never need to worry about your finances ever again. All your financial needs are taken care of by the contents of this trunk.

How do you feel? What thoughts are going through your head at this moment? Are you thrilled? Or are your nervous? Are there any negative emotions associated with receiving this trunk or its contents? Do you have any questions about the money?

You may now open your eyes.

I used this exercise to discover how Susan really felt about being wealthy or rich. Something surprising occurred as I went through this exercise with her. When Susan opened the trunk and saw all of that money, she physically shuddered. When the exercise was over, I asked her why.

"It scared me," she replied.

"LOOK AT YOUR THOUGHTS ABOUT MONEY AND START CHANGING YOUR THOUGHTS. THE MONEY WILL THEN RESPOND DIFFERENTLY."

-- FREDRIC LEHRMAN

"So, you want lots of money but, at the same time, having a lot of money scares you, is that right?"

Susan wanted to be wealthy but large amounts of money scared her for some reason. I explained to her that she would never become wealthy until she understood and overcame her fear of money.

So, I don't know why everyone isn't a millionaire, but I do know why Susan isn't. She is afraid of large sums of money. Please keep in mind that Susan's fear did not come out of the trunk of money. It came out of her own thoughts about the money.

We need to examine our own mental beliefs about money in order to effectively control the flow of wealth in and around our lives. Does the thought of having large sums of money bother you in some way? What problems do you imagine a trunk full of money could create for you?

What were you taught to believe about money and your relationship with it? Were you told that money doesn't grow on trees? Do you believe that money is the root of all evil? Or, like me, were you told that there isn't enough money for the things you desire? Keep in mind that there are no problems in that trunk. The problems are only in your mind.

In my childhood, I learned that there was never enough money at the end of the month and so frivolous desires and other unnecessary comforts must be forgone. In my adult life, I lived with this same belief. I began to do an exercise similar to Mr. Lehrman's Trunk Full of Money exercise. I attempted to use this technique to produce a quarter million dollars, or a half million dollars and I had absolutely no success whatsoever. What I did produce was an astounding learning experience that has brought me greater financial success than I think I could have ever attained without the benefit of subconscious communication.

I used to go on a walk every morning and visualize that I had found a briefcase or a bag or something that contained an exorbitant amount of money and no identifying marks of its original owner. I never even found a loose dollar bill lying in the gutter among the leaves. At one point in my life, I decided to stop looking for hundreds of thousands of dollars and simply concentrate on my immediate needs at hand.

At the time, I figured that I needed to raise eight thousand dollars. So, on my morning walks, I began to visualize finding a briefcase or a bag with eight thousand dollars in it. I never found a bag of money but, interestingly, within a month of visualizing myself finding the money I currently needed, I received two unexpected and unsolicited checks. One check was for five thousand dollars. The other check was for $3,360.00. Neither of these checks were the result of something I had earned or because of something I had sold. They were both, quite literally, unexpected gifts from the universe.

So, perhaps we shouldn't all be seeking to become millionaires through our subconscious activities. Perhaps a more effective tool in shaping our financial lives would be simply looking to have our present needs, wants and desires met and taken care of. Then, as we begin to expand our thinking, we can also begin to expand our financial desires.

Opening the Windows

I believe in the concept of paying a tithe and I have experienced some interesting results associated with tithing. Fredric Lehrman teaches that tithing began as an agricultural process, where farmers would hold back ten percent of their harvest to be used to seed the following season's harvest. I believe that tithing is a spiritually based principle.

In the Old Testament, the prophet Malachi advises us to "bring the entire tithe into the storehouse" as a test to see whether God will "open for you the windows of heaven and pour out for you a blessing until there is no room for it all."

I was raised with the idea that if I paid tithing, then God would take care of my needs and this was all that I ever really expected or hoped for. Tithing, for me, is an expression of gratitude, a way of thanking God, or thanking the universe, by returning a portion of what we receive back to God, whether that be through a charity or a church or some other benevolent organization. I do not consider offering a tithe as a bargaining tool where we tell God (or the universe) "I'll do this if you'll do that."

Nonetheless, Malachi's words seemed like a very promising and worthwhile effort and I have used it with amazing results. The idea of paying tithing, however, with the intention of getting something in return was foreign to me.

When I was in my late teens, I attended a conference where I heard a speaker discuss the topic of tithing. This gentleman told his audience that, "If you are earning fifty thousand dollars a year and you want to earn a hundred thousand dollars a year, then pay tithing on a hundred thousand dollars. Within a year you will be earning a hundred thousand dollars a year."

I had a difficult time processing this information. I could not accept the idea that if someone were to double their tithing, then they would double their income within a year. This couldn't be true because, if it were, everyone would do it. Consequently, I dismissed the idea immediately and entirely. It simply couldn't work.

But the thought came back to me about fifteen years later. I had just secured a job as a full-time public relations writer for a company in Los Angeles. I purchased a home and moved my family there and things were going extremely well. In my interview upon accepting the position I was told that after one year I would be given a four percent increase in pay. It was ardently emphasized that it wouldn't be sooner than one year, and it wouldn't be more than four percent. I was fine with this. I had just landed the best paying job of my career so far.

Living in this new environment I wasn't as involved in spiritual activities as much as I had been previously and wanted to do more but I didn't know where to begin. The thought occurred to me that I could at least increase my tithe offering as a way of benefiting the community I was now living in. This was the moment I remembered the speaker at the conference I had attended. I wasn't particularly interested in doubling my income over the next year, but still felt that doubling my tithing would be valuable and appropriate. Accordingly, the following Sunday, I doubled my donation to the church I attended. I thought nothing more about it. It was a simple and insignificant gesture on my part but one that I hoped would somehow keep me connected with my spirituality.

Wednesday morning my boss, the Director of the company I worked for, called me to his office. I had been working there about six months now. He informed me that the Board of Directors had noticed the work I was doing, and they were pleased with the results. He said that they wanted to reward me and that, beginning immediately, they offered to double my salary. I was astounded but also a little confused.

I reminded my boss, "You told me—emphatically—one year, four percent. That was all I could expect."

"Well," he said, "the Board of Directors feels differently now."

I went back to my office to consider what had just happened. It was far too much of a coincidence to be coincidental. On Sunday I doubled my tithing, on Wednesday I doubled my income. Then I suddenly realized I was faced with a dilemma; do I continue to double my tithing donation, or do I go back to the customary ten percent?

I determined that I had made a commitment to double my donation and that I would continue with that determination. For the next two months I doubled my tithing. By the third month the Board of Directors decided to raise my salary once more—again doubling my income. In the course of three months I had quadrupled my income at a company that had assured me that I would only receive a four percent increase after one year.

Do you remember what I told you about Susan being frightened by large sums of money? This still seems strange for me to say but doubling my income twice in three months frightened me. I felt a sense of power that I was not used to, and it made me extremely uncomfortable. Consequently, I stopped doubling my tithing and went back to the accustomed ten percent. I continued to receive increases in my salary over the ten years I worked at that company but nothing as dramatic and staggering as quadrupling my income in three months' time.

Mr. Lehrman expresses that paying tithing is an indication to the subconscious mind that there is more than enough money to cover all of your needs, wants and desires. If your subconscious is convinced that there is more than enough, it will make certain to provide you with more than enough.

When Fredric Lehrman began to work systematically on the changes we have been discussing in this book, he increased his income *sixteen* times in one year! He also discovered that these concepts are so intrinsic in our society that anyone can do this.

Perhaps, like me, you have doubts. Keep in mind that those doubts are just thoughts. Those thoughts have reasons. They are based on earlier thoughts that take precedence. When you think, "Oh, it's just a thought," then you disregard the immense power thoughts have over our lives and our actions.

"THOUGHT IS THE ORIGINAL SOURCE OF ALL WEALTH, ALL SUCCESS, ALL MATERIAL GAIN, ALL GREAT DISCOVERIES AND INVENTIONS, AND OF ALL ACHIEVEMENT."

-- CLAUDE M BRISTOL

Paying the Bills

A simple experiment can show how the power of the subconscious can be involved in your finances. If you are skeptical, as I was, you can try this experiment. Anyone can do this without added financial risk. It simply involves paying the bills which we all have to do anyway.

Mr. Lehrman suggests taking a bill—*this must be a bill that you already have the money to pay*—and placing that bill on the mantle above the fireplace or taped to the refrigerator door or somewhere conspicuous where you will see it often. Do this a couple of weeks before the bill is due.

Then, do not immediately pay this bill. Instead, ask your subconscious to bring you the money to pay it. Whenever you see the bill, trust that the universe is sending you that money.

This is one of the first financial experiments I performed with my subconscious mind. The bill was for $426.00. I had the money to pay it but instead, I placed the bill on the mantle in my home. I felt a great deal of skepticism. No one owed me money. I couldn't imagine where this $426.00 would come from. But I thought it was still worth a try.

Several days before the bill was due, I received an adjustment on my income tax for $386.00. This was totally unexpected and, although it didn't completely cover the amount of the bill on my mantle, it certainly came close to it.

If you attempt this experiment with a bill that you DO NOT have the finances to pay already in hand, it will create too much tension in your subconscious mind. Your concern and worry over whether the money will actually show up will create the opposite effect. Worry, concern and doubt are opposing mental forces that block you from manifesting what you truly desire. For this experiment to work it must be with a bill that you can already afford to pay. That way there is no anxiety or internal conflict challenging your attention or intention.

I don't want to create doubt for you, but I cannot guarantee that this will work every time. So, what if it works eighty percent of the time? Wouldn't that be an exceptional improvement? Even if it only worked fifty percent of the time, half of your bills would be taken care of. And what if it worked only twenty percent of the time? Would you be willing to have your subconscious mind take care of twenty percent of your bills?

I still continue this practice today. In fact, the same morning that I wrote this chapter, I placed the bill for our car payment on the mantle above the fireplace. I have full confidence that the money to make that payment is already on its way.

I believe this is a much healthier and a more effective exercise than asking the universe to send me a million dollars.

The Lehrman Project

CHAPTER EIGHT

YOUR INNER DIALOGUE

Growing up I was never very kind or complimentary in the way in which I talked to myself. I was harsh and extremely judgmental in my inner dialogues. One day an acquaintance asked me, "If you spoke to a friend in the same way that you speak to yourself, how long would you have that friend?"

For me, this was a very eye-opening statement. Consider it for a moment. How do you talk to yourself? Are you complimentary, encouraging and kind or are you cruel, demanding and critical in your internal discussions?

I have discovered that the most important dialogue you have in any given day is the dialogue you have with yourself. Those little children in your subconscious mind, whether you are aware of them are not, are very eager to please you and comply with your requests. If you tell yourself, "I'm such an idiot," then these anxious and eager little children are going to rush off to comply with the image you have just verbally created for them. They are going to go out into the universe to bring you proof that you are an idiot. (Don't blame them. They're only acting on your command.)

I referenced my father in Chapter Two and his inability to remember names. Once he changed his inner dialogue from "I can't remember his name…" to "His name will come to me in a minute," his ability to remember names changed dramatically.

Lately, in my own experience, I am constantly dropping things. Whenever this happened, I would say to myself, "Why am I always dropping things?" I began to wonder if my inner dialogue was re-enforcing my unwanted behavior. I decided to change the conversation within myself. Now, if I drop something, I say, "Wow. That *never* happens to me."

I have noticed a marked decline in the number of times I drop something now.

You may wonder if what you say in your inner dialogue can really have any effect on the physical world around you. We discussed in Chapter Two how we can feel differently around different people for no apparent reason and how other people are reacting toward us in a similar fashion. All of this is because of subliminal conversations that we are all having within ourselves. Refining our inner dialogue and learning how to talk to ourselves effectively and profitably, will definitely affect our environment as well as our relationships.

All of this is very subjective, I know, but it can also be proven. In Chapter One of this book, I discussed the experiment my father conducted with the second-hand of his watch sweeping the twelve.

"IF YOU FORM A PICTURE IN YOUR MIND OF WHAT YOU WOULD LIKE TO BE, AND YOU KEEP AND HOLD THAT PICTURE THERE LONG ENOUGH, YOU WILL SOON BECOME EXACTLY AS YOU HAVE BEEN THINKING."

-- WILLIAM JAMES

He had no way of knowing when the second-hand would be on the twelve, but he trusted that anytime he looked at his watch, the second-hand would be sweeping the twelve.

If our thoughts can affect how we respond to something as physical as a wristwatch, then doubtlessly our thoughts can affect how we respond to other things such as money, people, and all sorts of circumstances within our own lives. It certainly stands out that our inner dialogue, our thoughts and conversations with the subconscious, are taken seriously by the little children running around inside our minds.

Tabula Rasa

The concept of the tabula rasa or blank slate proposes we all enter the world with absolutely no pre-formed thoughts or ideas. Everything we think and feel is learned in childhood. Our minds are like a blank chalk board that is written upon by every passing person and experience we go through in life. We become the sum total of everything we learn, feel, and experience growing up.

One of the most significant discoveries in the field of human potential is the idea of the self-concept. We develop a bundle of beliefs regarding ourselves, beginning at birth. Our self-concept becomes the master program of our subconscious mind, determining everything we think, say, feel, and do. What we do and become as adults later in life is the result of this early conditioning.

I remember when I was a young child standing in the parking lot at school. A man walked by me. He might have been a teenager, or he might have been an adult, but to a little child like me he was just a 'grown-up.' As he walked past me, he remarked, "How could someone as intelligent as your father have a kid as stupid as you?"

A couple of things happened in my mind. First of all, I didn't know who this person was, but he obviously knew me and my dad since he was accurate in his assessment of my father being intelligent. Secondly, if he was correct in his assessment of my father, then he must also be correct in his assessment about me. If some grown-up I don't even know believes that I am stupid, then I must really be stupid was the inevitable conclusion I drew.

I'm certain it wasn't due to this circumstance alone, but I grew up thinking and believing that I was stupid. In elementary school my grades reflected and reinforced that belief in me. However, when I was in high school, I accidentally took an English class intended for advanced students only. On the first day of class when the teacher announced that the course was for advanced students, I immediately thought of dropping out. Instead, I decided to stick it out.

Thanks to a wonderful teacher and a lot of hard work on my part, I passed the course with a perfect score. My world began to change. My GPA for the last two years of high school and the first two years of college was 4.0. Despite this remarkable change, I still believed I was stupid.

"YOU ARE NOT WHAT YOU THINK YOU ARE, BUT WHAT YOU THINK, YOU ARE."

-- BRIAN TRACEY

One afternoon I was talking to a counselor at the University and I commented to him that I wasn't very intelligent. He said, "What are you talking about?" I told him that I have never been an intelligent person. He took my file from one of his drawers and opened it to an IQ test I had taken upon enrollment. I had never seen the results of the test, but the counselor showed me that I had scored above the genius level.

If I hadn't seen the test results, I wouldn't have believed it. In *my* mind I knew I was stupid. It was an image I had carried with me from my childhood. Good grades and high-test scores couldn't change the image I held of myself. I had to return to my subconscious mind and erase the messages that had been written on my chalkboard many years ago and replace them with newer, more accurate images.

When you believe something to be true, it becomes true for you, no matter what the facts may indicate to the contrary. Everything you are today is the result of an idea or impression you took in and accepted as true. Every idea, opinion, feeling, attitude, or value you have as an adult you learned from childhood. All outward change occurs when you change your inner perception of yourself. When you change the way you think and feel about yourself and your world, then the world around you changes.

On some level in our subconscious thinking we have this approach to life that nothing is easy and that good things come only with great effort. We say things like, "No pain, no gain." We believe that nothing in life is simple. We feel that life is meant to be a struggle. These ideas and these clever little phrases which we have been taught from childhood have become habitual.

The truth is, these habitual belief systems are keeping you in a pattern of making your life difficult. We have layers of protective thoughts that keep us locked in place and prevent us from moving forward. Fredric Lehrman makes the radical suggestion that it is safe to have things be easy. It is safe for your life to function smoothly. And it can happen as we change the quality of our internal communication.

The Lehrman Project

CHAPTER NINE

A GREAT MIRROR

When you communicate with the subconscious mind continuously about the results you want in your life, whether or not you feel these methods are ridiculous, silly, or just plain crazy, your way of thinking will soon become habitual. The more you communicate what you want to the children of your subconscious, the more your mind will seek out and deliver to you the life that you are looking for. The more this happens, the more purposeful, confident and creative you will become.

Our main task and concern should be to create the mental image *within* of the life we desire *without*. What we impress on the inside, we express on the outside. By activating the power of the subconscious mind, we can attract the forces of the universe to work on our behalf. By directing and instructing the child mind, we take control of our own lives and experiences.

We become what we most think about and our outer world is merely the reflection of what we are thinking about in our inner world. When we change our method of thinking, we change our lives. It is that simple.

Happy, successful, positive people think about what they want and how to get it most of the time. Unhappy, unsuccessful, negative people think about what they don't want.

Perhaps the most important quality you can develop to achieve greater success and happiness in life is the quality of optimal inner communication. You can learn to use the power of your subconscious mind the same way prosperous and cheerful people constantly and continuously use their minds to create prosperity, abundance and joy.

Mental exertion is very similar to physical exertion. It takes a portion of our time and it takes effort to achieve and maintain our mental skills and abilities. I hope that I have demonstrated that the effort is definitely worth the results. The reward can be extraordinary!

Progress may be slow at first in some areas. It isn't always a smooth transition from your old way of thinking to the ideal of creating a clear image of the life, career, relationships or financial circumstances you would like to experience. If you persist, if you continually work on improving your inner communication with your subconscious mind, you will achieve the results proportional to the efforts you give it.

There are certain specific subjects that the most contented, successful and positive people think about the majority of the time. The more your thoughts reflect on these ideas, the more your outer world will mirror your inner desires.

"THE WORLD IS LIKE A GREAT MIRROR. IT REFLECTS BACK TO YOU WHAT YOU ARE. IF YOU ARE LOVING, IF YOU ARE FRIENDLY, IF YOU ARE HELPFUL, THE WORLD WILL PROVE LOVING, FRIENDLY, AND HELPFUL TO YOU. THE WORLD IS WHAT YOU ARE."

-- THOMAS DREIER

Think about the results you want to achieve. Work towards being effective and efficient at getting the results you desire.

1. Think about the things you desire, the goals you have and the things you want to accomplish.

2. Think positively about your future. Do not dwell on the past.

3. Think about doing things in a better way. Don't become trapped in antiquated ideas or childhood programming that isn't elevating or enriching.

4. Think about solutions. Don't focus all your mental energy on the problems. What you most think about, you will create.

5. Think about what you can do. Think about the next step you can take to reach the life you want.

6. Think about what you are thinking about. Pay attention to your thoughts and the direction

they are leading you. Evict thoughts that do not create value.

When you perfect your inner dialogue, when you begin to communicate effectively with your own subconscious and then extend that communication to the subconscious minds of others, then there are no real limits to what you can be, what you can do, and what you can have. There is almost nothing that you cannot be, do or have if you want it passionately and powerfully enough and work toward it. You can create a garden of thoughts within your own mind that will continually grow into the harvest you are seeking. You can use the ideas in this book to improve your life daily and to create greater happiness and success for the rest of your life. Your potential is unlimited, and your possibilities are endless. The key is to begin today, and then never give up.

The Lehrman Project

"WE ARE LIVING IN THE GOLDEN AGE OF MANKIND. THERE HAVE NEVER BEEN MORE OPPORTUNITIES AND POSSIBILITIES FOR YOU TO BECOME ALL YOU ARE CAPABLE OF BECOMING, AND TO ACHIEVE MORE OF YOUR GOALS, THAN THERE ARE TODAY."

-- BRIAN TRACEY

ABOUT THE AUTHOR:

Steven Claysen was born in a small farming town near Columbus, Ohio. As a young boy he began studying the power of thought after reading James Allen's classic little book, *"As a Man Thinketh."* He became an avid reader and student of creative thinking. He used the power of creative thinking to improve his relationships, find the right jobs, and create wealth.

He is the founder of Deep End Enterprises, a third-tier marketing company. He also worked as a debt consultant and financial advisor at Boardwalk Financial Services.

www.stevenclaysen.com

The Lehrman Project

ALSO BY STEVEN CLAYSEN:

THE POWER OF ATTRACTION:

HOW TO APPLY THE LAW OF ATTRACTION TO CREATE THE LIFE YOU WANT

The Power of Attraction is no secret. It is the power of love. Love creates. Love binds. Love is powerful energy.

One expression of love is desire. Attach desire to any thought and believe in its reality and it will manifest itself.

Every thought, every feeling, every action you take causes a reaction. You are at cause. You have this power within you. You use it constantly, either deliberately with deliberate results or unintentionally with unintended and random results.

If any aspect of your life isn't what you hoped it would be, then this book can help you. *The Power of Attraction* contains proven steps and strategies on how to create the life you want through practical application of the Law of

Attraction. This book will show you how to apply the Law of Attraction to help you attain the positive things you are looking for; improved relationships, better circumstances, increased prosperity, greater joy, etc.

www.ingramcontent.com/pod-product-compliance
Lightning Source LLC
Chambersburg PA
CBHW070933210326
41520CB00021B/6925